Pooh's Potful of Fun

Walt Disney
Productions'

Pooh's
Potful of Fun

PURNELL
ISBN 0 361 05325 8
Copyright © Walt Disney Productions
Published 1981 by Purnell Books, Paulton,
Bristol BS18 5LQ, a member of the BPCC group of companies.
Printed in Great Britain
by Purnell and Sons Limited
Stories in this book are derived from the
Winnie-the-Pooh books written by A. A. Milne with
illustrations by E. H. Shepard; published in the
United Kingdom by Methuen and Co. Ltd.

CONTENTS

Pooh's Favourite Photo

If you want Pooh to see a picture of you, just stick a photograph of yourself in the picture frame.

STICK YOUR

Where is Everyone?

It is a rainy day in the Hundred Acre Wood and no one seems to be around. Here is a picture of Pooh's house. If you hold the page up to the light, you will see where everyone is.

Christopher Robin's New Yellow Cap

One blustery day Christopher Robin wore his new
yellow cap. The pictures below show what happened to him
and his cap. The pictures are not in the correct order,
however. Can you tell which picture should be first,
second, third, and fourth?

Who's Who

It's late at night and everyone is coming home from a party at Christopher Robin's house. Can you tell who's who in the dark?

Try to guess and then turn the book upside down to see how well you did.

Kanga

Piglet

Pooh

Roo

Tigger

Owl

Eeyore

Rabbit

11

Winnie-the-Pooh's "I Spy" Game

Winnie-the-Pooh loves to play "I Spy". You will, too. At least two players are needed for the game. The one who is IT looks around and picks an object that he or she sees. The object must be within view of both players. IT does not say what the object is. IT just says: "I spy with my little eye something that is blue." (The player can choose any object of any colour.)

Now the second player must look around and try to guess the object. When the second player guesses correctly, it is his or her turn to be IT.

See if you can guess what Winnie-the-Pooh spies. He says: "I spy with my little eye something that is brown!"

THIS IS FOR TRACING

A

FOLD   FOLD

Make a Twirly Whirly

Piglet and Rabbit have made Twirly Whirlys that spin around and around.

Here is how you can make one: First, on a sheet of paper, trace the Twirly Whirly shape on the opposite page. Make sure you include line A and the dotted line also. Then cut out the shape you have traced.

Cut along line A also and stop when you reach the dotted line. Now, fold back the wings in opposite directions as shown below.

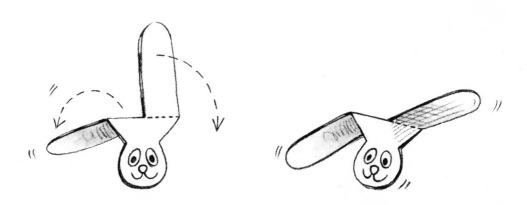

Turn the page to see what to do next.

Take a long piece of string. Stick it to the end of the Twirly Whirly as shown.

To make your Twirly Whirly fly and flutter, just hold the string in your hand and move the Twirly Whirly back and forth through the air as Rabbit is doing.

Owl's Memory Game

Owl has a very good memory, as he often tells everyone. Here's a memory game you can play by yourself. All you have to do is study the pictures on this page carefully. Try to remember everything you see.

Now turn the page and answer Owl's questions.

Tigger

Piglet

Pooh

Rabbit

Roo

Kanga

Eeyore

17

Owl's Questions:
(Remember now, answer the questions without peeping back!)

1. What is Rabbit holding in his hand?
2. What is Piglet playing with?
3. Who is riding on top of Eeyore?
4. What is Tigger doing?
5. What is Kanga using?
6. What is Pooh eating?

Rabbit's Relations

Rabbit has lots and lots of relations. How many of them can you find on this page?

Hidden Animals

Christopher Robin, Sir Brian, and Dragon are playing "Hidden Animals."

Here is how the game goes: In each word below there is the name of an animal. For instance, in the word PLANT there is an ANT (PL<u>ANT</u>). See if you can find the animals in the other words below.

1. PLANT
2. PIGMENT
3. COWBOY
4. THEN

5. CROWN
6. SCAT
7. BOWL
8. BEET

What Begins With "B"?

Study the picture of Kanga cleaning her house and see how many objects you can find that begin with the letter "B". On a separate piece of paper, you may want to make a list of all the objects you find.

What's Missing?

Here are two pictures of Sir Brian and Dragon in front of Sir Brian's castle. At first glance both pictures look alike. But in the picture on page 23 there are ten things missing. Can you discover what they are?

Famous Trick

Christopher Robin is holding a picture of a magician with long whiskers. This magician's most famous trick is pulling a rabbit out of his hat. (Not Pooh's friend Rabbit, of course!) To see the famous trick, turn the page upside down.

Piglet's and Roo's Friends

Piglet and Roo are making little make-believe friends all by themselves.

So can you, and here is how: Next time you find some acorns or flat stones in the woods, or anywhere else, take them home with you. With a felt-tip pen, draw eyes and a mouth on each acorn or stone.

You can make as many little friends as you like!

Twin Poohs

Even when Pooh is flying his kite, he takes a honey jar along just in case he needs a little snack.

Here are six pictures of Pooh flying his kite, but only two of them are exactly alike. Can you tell which two they are?

A B C

D E F

Rabbit's Magic Carrot

Rabbit asks if you have ever seen a *blue* carrot with *red* leaves. Perhaps not. But if you would like to perform a little magic with your eyes, you can make the carrot below turn to orange and the leaves to green.

Here's how: Just stare at the black dot on the carrot while you slowly count to fifty. Then blink your eyes rapidly and look at a blank white space such as a wall or piece of paper. You should see an orange carrot with green leaves!

Pin the Tail on Eeyore!

Poor Eeyore has lost his tail again. Wouldn't you know! Play this game and help Eeyore to get his tail back.

Here is what to do: Take a sheet of paper large enough to trace the picture of Eeyore on pages 30 and 31. Make sure you include the star. Colour the picture with your crayons and then stick it to a wall. Next, take a sheet of loose-leaf paper and trace as many tails as you need for players. (The pattern is on page 30.) Colour the tails too and cut them out along their outlines.

Take a small piece of sticky tape and roll it up with the sticky side facing out, as shown. Stick the roll on the back of the tail. Make as many rolls as you need and stick one on each tail.

You are now ready to play. Blindfold each player in turn and give him or her a tail. The winner is the person who sticks the tail closest to the star on Eeyore.

Sticky Side Out

FOR
TRACING
EEYORE
AND
EEYORE'S
TAIL

Winnie-the-Pooh and Piglet Dolls

Winnie-the-Pooh and Piglet are two of Christopher Robin's favourite playmates, and they can be your playmates, too, because they're easy to make. Just follow the simple steps. Directions for making the Pooh doll are given on this page and on page 33. Directions for making the Piglet doll are on pages 36 and 37.

Take a sheet of paper and trace the FRONT part of Pooh from the pattern on page 34. Take another sheet of paper and do the same thing with the BACK part from the pattern on page 35. (Use a thick, soft pencil or a black crayon for best results.)

Next, colour the two traced pieces with crayon. Then cut them out. Be sure you don't cut out the space between Pooh's feet, or he won't stand up.

Stick the FRONT and BACK parts together with bits of tape on the outside as shown below.

Leave the bottom part open, however.

Now take bits of tissue paper or cotton wool and stuff them inside the two parts until Pooh is nice and fat. Your stuffed Pooh is finished! You can tape up the bottom part or leave it open so that Pooh can stand.

Now see pages 36 and 37 for how to make Piglet.

THIS IS FOR TRACING

THIS IS FOR TRACING

To make a Piglet doll, trace the FRONT part from the pattern on page 38. Do the same thing with the BACK part from the pattern on page 39.

Colour the two pieces you have traced. Next, cut them out. Be sure you don't cut out the space between Piglet's feet, or he won't stand up.

Stick the FRONT and BACK parts together with bits of tape on the outside as shown below.

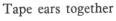

Tape ears together

Tape feet together

Next stuff Piglet with bits of tissue paper or cotton wool as you did with Pooh. Tape up the bottom part of Piglet or leave it open so that he can stand.

Now you have your very own Pooh and Piglet dolls.

THIS IS FOR TRACING

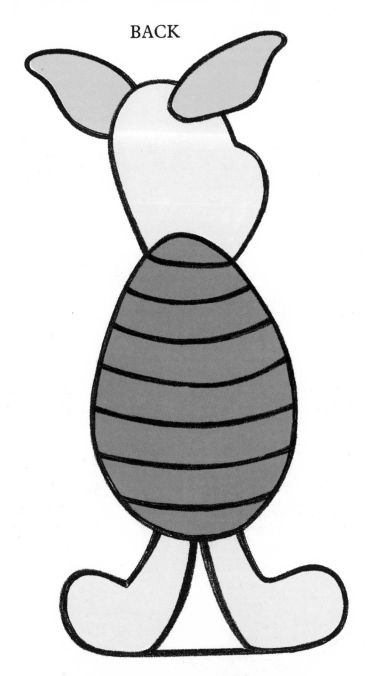

THIS IS FOR TRACING

Find the Mistakes

Here is a funny picture with Pooh, Piglet, and Roo. There are ten silly mistakes. Can you find them?

Where Are Roo and Piglet?

Kanga is looking for Roo and Piglet. They were playing by the tree a minute ago, but now she can't find them. Look very closely at the picture and try to find Roo and Piglet. They are hidden in it somewhere.

What Begins With "C"?

Here is a comfortable, cosy picture of the inside of Pooh's house. See how many objects you can find that begin with the letter "C". You may want to make a list on a separate piece of paper of the objects as you find them.

Count Pooh's Honey Pots

Pooh keeps lots of honey in his house because it is his favourite food. How many honey pots can you count in Pooh's house?

Make a Picture of You

Christopher Robin, Piglet, and Roo are going to show you how to make a picture of YOU!

You will need a large sheet of plain wrapping paper, scissors, and a black crayon.

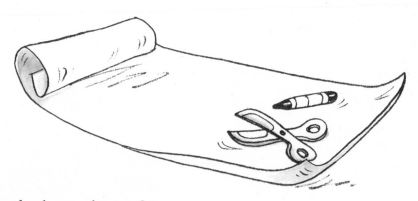

Place the large sheet of paper on the floor. Now, lie down on the paper (as Christopher Robin is doing) and ask a friend to trace the outline of your body with the crayon straight on to the paper.

Colour your portrait and add
as many details as you like
(eyes, nose, mouth, hair, etc.).

Then cut out YOU and hang
YOU up!

Christopher Robin's Pirate Treasure Hunt

Christopher Robin is playing "Pirate Treasure Hunt" with Piglet. You can play with a friend, too. It's easy. All you have to do is to hide a small object somewhere indoors or outdoors. Then draw a map of where you hid it. The map can be very simple, with stick figures for chairs, or trees, or anything else. You can even label the figures on your map. Then draw a big X where the object is hidden.

Now give the map to your friend and tell him or her to find the "treasure". After the person has found the object, it's his or her turn to hide some treasure and draw a map.

Kanga's Tea Party Game

At first glance the pictures on pages 48 and 49 look alike.
But in the picture on page 49 there are ten things missing.
Do you know what they are?

49

Tigger's Bouncing Game

You can play Tigger's bouncing game by yourself or with another player.

Pick a star, and with the rubber end of a pencil follow the line from that star as it bounces on the ground and then against the tree. The number on the tree is your score. If you are playing by yourself, you can win if you hit all three number 5s in four "turns" or less. If you are playing with another person, take it in turns to pick a star. Whoever gets the highest score after all the stars have been picked is the winner. Remember, it wouldn't be fair to follow a line before you picked a star.

Happy-Sad Pooh

When Pooh has a full jar of honey, he's happy.
After he has eaten all his honey, he's sad.

See how Pooh looks before and after. First cover the
right side of the picture with a piece of paper on the dotted
line. Then cover the left side in the same way.

Rhyme Time

Pooh loves to make up rhymes. He wants to help you make up rhymes, too. Pooh says name the ten pictures below. Then match the words that rhyme with each other.

Here's a rhyme that Pooh made from a pair of rhyming words below.

I'm going to follow that little bee.
I hope he takes me to a honey tree.

Now see what rhymes you can make.
Before you know it, you'll be a poet.

Play Hide-and-Seek With Rabbit

Pooh, Christopher Robin, and Rabbit are playing a game of hide-and-seek. Rabbit is going to hide in one of his holes and Pooh and Christopher Robin have to try to find him. If you would like to join in the game, you can. You will need a teacup, a sheet of black stiff paper, a pencil, a ten-pence piece, a piece of white paper, and a pair of scissors.

First, trace three circles of the teacup on the black paper as shown below. Cut out the circles you have traced. These will be Rabbit's holes.

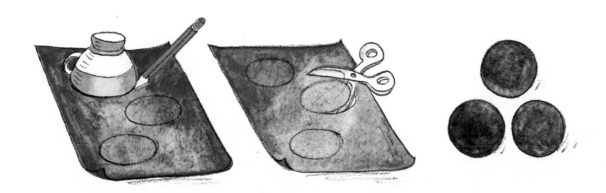

Next, trace a circle of the ten-pence piece on the white paper. Add two ears and a face as shown below. This will be Rabbit. Make sure that Rabbit's ears aren't too long and that he is smaller than the black circles. Cut out the figure of Rabbit.

Now you are ready to play. Remember that it takes two people to play this game. Turn to the next page and you will see how to do it.

Place the black circles on a table. One player closes his eyes and counts to ten while the other hides Rabbit under one of the black circles. Now try to guess which circle Rabbit is under. You have only one guess. After you have had your guess, it is the other person's turn to close his eyes and count to ten while you hide Rabbit.

The first person to get three correct guesses is the winner of the game.

Twin Dragons

In the pictures of Dragon below, there are only two that are exactly alike. Can you see which two they are?

The End

Below are four pictures of Pooh and a sign that he has made just for you. The pictures are not in the correct order, however. Can you put them in the correct order and say which pictures should be first, second, third, and fourth?

Answers

p. 9
Christopher Robin's New
Yellow Cap
D, A, B, C

p. 19
Rabbit's Relations
12 rabbits

p. 20
1. PLANT   5. CROWN
2. PIGMENT   6. SCAT
3. COWBOY   7. BOWL
4. THEN   8. BEET

p. 21
What Begins With "B"?
ball, blocks, box, bird, bird
cage, books, butterfly, bee,
bag, basket, boots, bread, *branch*
bottle, bananas, brush, bucket,
bubbles, broom

black, brown, blue,

p. 22
What's Missing?
1. bird 2. Piglet's stripes 3. Sir
Brian's stripe on tunic 4. one
of Dragon's scales 5. fish in moat
6. doorknob. 7. one of stakes
above door 8. sun 9. Dragon's
hat 10. candle in window

p. 26
Twin Poohs   A and F

p. 40
Find the Mistakes
1. doorknob is in middle of
door 2. cart has one square
wheel 3. bird is in fish bowl
4. Roo has Tigger's tail 5. no
picture in frame 6. candle in
lantern is upside down
7. Pooh's book is upside down
8. fish is in bird cage 9. sun
and stars are out together
10. Pooh's chair has square leg

p. 41
Where Are Roo and Piglet?

p. 42
What Begins With 'C'?
cheese, cake, camera, coat,
curtains, candle, cupboard,
chair, cherry, clock, cobweb

p. 43
Count Pooh's Honey Pots
15 honey pots

p. 48
Kanga's Tea Party Game
1. Piglet's cup 2. lampshade
3. Pooh's honey pot 4. rain in
window 5. clock face

6. flowers in pot 7. Kanga's tail
8. Eeyore's ribbon on tail
9. rug 10. a cupcake

p. 53
Rhyme Time
Pooh—Roo, bee—tree,
Dragon—wagon, moon—
spoon, honey—money

p. 57
Twin Dragons
B and D

p. 58
The End
B, A, D, C

SIR BRIAN'S CASTLE

RABBIT'S HOUSE

POOH'S HOUSE

SIX PINE TREES

PIGLET'S HOUSE

KANGA'S HOUSE

SAND PIT